Published by Creative Education
123 South Broad Street, Mankato, Minnesota 56001
Creative Education is an imprint of The Creative Company

Designed by Stephanie Blumenthal
Production Design by Melinda Belter

Photographs by Frank S. Balthis, David F. Clobes, Faribo Woolen Mills,
Galyn C. Hammond, Grant Heilman Photography, Inc./John Colwell, D.J.
Lambrecht, Craig Lovell, Leslie M. Newman,
Chuck Place, Lior Rubin, Edmond Van Hoorick

Library of Congress Cataloging-in-Publication Data

Healy-Johnson, Guinevere, 1967–
Wool / by Guinevere Healy-Johnson
p. cm. — (Let's Investigate)
Includes glossary
Summary: Examines the origins, processing, and historical and modern
uses of various kinds of wool.
ISBN 0-88682-965-8
1. Wool—Juvenile literature. [1. Wool.] I. Title. II. Series. III. Series:
Let's Investigate (Mankato, Minn.)
TS1547.H43   1999
677'.31—dc21   98-30296

First edition

2 4 6 8 9 7 5 3 1

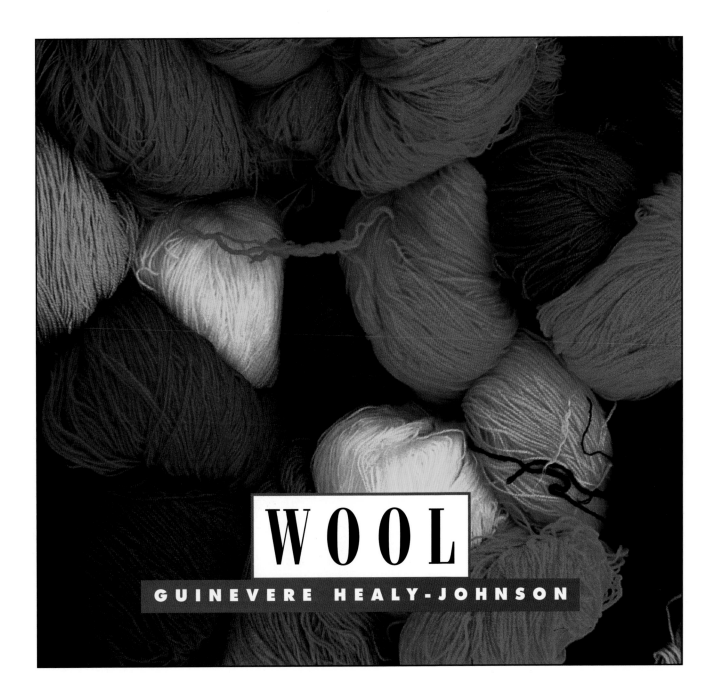

WOOL

GUINEVERE HEALY-JOHNSON

Creative ☾ Education

WOOL

*Wool can soak up as much as one-third of its own weight in moisture before it gets wet. Even damp wool **insulates.***

Right, Navajo rug
Below, llama coats are a source of wool

4

W

hile not much is the same as it was 6,000 years ago, one thing has not changed. People still make products from wool. A natural fiber, wool comes from animals such as sheep, llamas, goats, and rabbits. Today, in factories around the world, everything from suits to carpeting and from cushions to curtains can be made from wool.

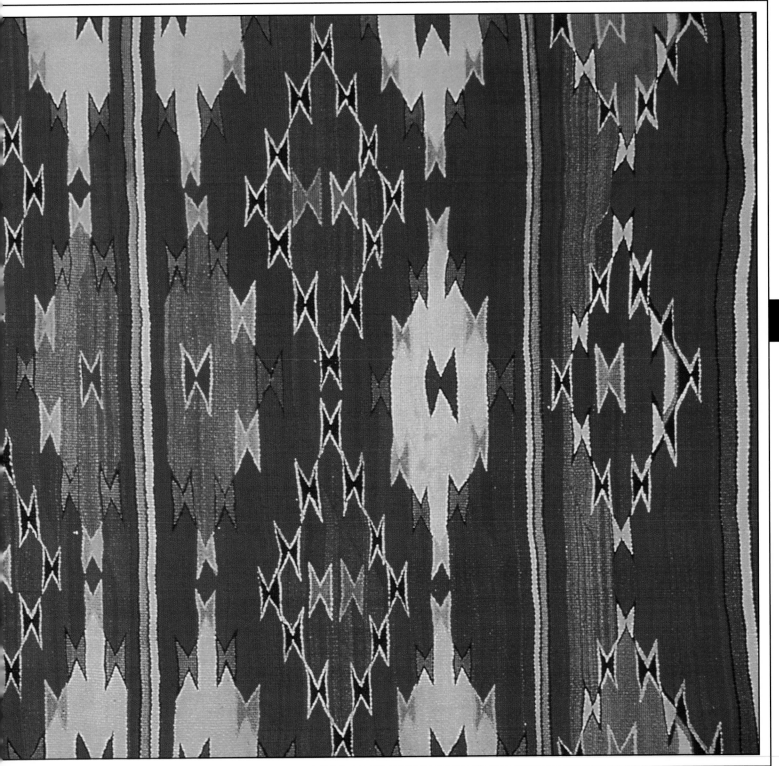

WOOL
SPORT

The fuzzy outsides of some tennis balls contain waste wool— any wool that can't be carded and spun into yarn.

WOOL
DOG

Sheepherding dogs, trained to help keep flocks of sheep to- gether, may run on the backs of the sheep to see all around the flock.

Sheep provide wool

WOOL'S SOURCES

Wool is the hairy under- coat of some animals such as sheep. Species of wild sheep have two layers of protection. The first is a short, wooly coat, and the second is a coat of coarse, long, straight hairs. **Domesticated** sheep do not have long overcoats like their wild relatives. Their wool is thicker and more dense.

A wool fiber, when examined under a microscope, looks like a worm with overlapping scales sticking out of it. No other fiber looks like this. It is more rough than other fibers, but it is the most stretchy of natural fibers (such as linen, cotton, and silk). When pulled out, a wool fiber becomes straight, but it pops back into a springy, curly shape when let go. The material is known for its **absorbency,** durability, and ability to insulate.

Waste wool is also used to make mattress stuffing and the outside of paint rollers and to give texture to some kinds of wallpaper.

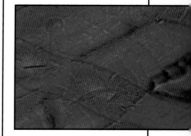

Above, microscopic wool fibers

WOOL

RECYCLE

Wool is a natural fiber. It is biodegradable, renewable, and recyclable.

WOOL

HISTORY

In 1609, American settlers brought sheep to Jamestown's colony in Virginia. The woolen fabrics they wove were called "homespuns."

Right, Angora sheep Opposite, freshly shorn sheep and lambs

Wool before it is processed is called fleece. Farmers shave the fleece off of the sheep once a year, most often in spring or summer. In areas where it is warm year-round, farmers may **shear** the sheep more than once. People use electric shavers or shears to cut the fleece off, close to the animal's skin. This does not hurt the sheep.

When fleece is shaved off of the sheep, it must be cleaned, classified, and processed before it can be made into the clothing and other products we use.

WOOL
MEAL

RAISING WOOL

Farmers raise sheep in nearly every country in the world. If sheep are well cared for, they can produce very nice wool. If they are not kept warm enough, not fed well, or otherwise not taken care of, they will produce hair and not wool.

Other animals, such as llamas, alpacas, vicuñas, **guanacos**, and even camels, produce wool. Cashmere comes from the Kasmir goat.

Top, sheep farmers often keep hundreds of animals
Bottom, llama farm in Oregon

ngora rabbits produce angora, and Angora goats produce mohair. Farmers collect fleece from these animals in much the same way as from sheep. Sometimes people just have to brush the rabbits to get their wool. Some of these animals do not produce as much fleece as sheep do. Thus this material is more rare and more expensive.

WOOL
DEFINITION

Clothing made from virgin wool contains 100 percent sheep wool; no fibers have been recycled from other products.

11

Wild vicuñas and alpacas in Chile, S. America

WOOL
CONTEST

*Most county and
state fairs in the U.S.
hold competitions for
sheep. Each animal
is judged on its ap-
pearance and the
quality of its coat.*

The world's largest wool producer is
Australia, which raises nearly 30 percent
of the world's supply. Other leading wool-
producing countries include Uruguay, New
Zealand,South Africa, China, Argentina, and
some of the former Soviet Republic countries.

***Above, trimming a sheep
for competition
Center, Angora rabbits***

The United States is not a leading wool producer. While huge Australian ranches can have 100,000 sheep, large ranches in the United States raise herds of 1,000 to 2,000 sheep. The United States **imports** all of its carpet wool and almost half of its clothing wool. While all states produce some wool, much of the United States' wool comes from Montana, Texas, Wyoming, Colorado, and South Dakota.

WOOL
GIANT

The one-humped dromedary camel, native to the deserts of the Middle East, is a source of wool; these animals can be seven feet (2 m) tall at the shoulder and weigh 1,500 pounds (680 kg).

Dromedary camel

WOOL
FINERY

Cashmere yarns spun in Scotland are some of the softest and finest of all wool. These are used for sweaters and shawls.

WOOL
DYE

Dyes were first made from plants and animals; the first man-made dye was invented in 1856—a purple color was created by coal tar.

Wool is dyed in many brilliant colors

WOOL'S FEATURES

Wool is a unique, dependable material that can be used in many ways and in many products. Its features give it an ease of use that cannot be claimed by many other fibers.

First, wool is an excellent insulator. It keeps people warm in the winter and cool in the summer. A wool sweater takes moisture away from the skin so that the body can retain its heat. Warmth is held in, staying close to the body in air pockets where it can do the most good. A light wool shirt pulls **perspiration** away from the skin, allowing the body to cool down. Wool's air pockets keep out hot air in warmer weather or cold air during cold weather.

WOOL GROWTH

The alpaca, a relative of the llama, must spend two years high in the Andes mountains in order to grow a complete coat of wool.

15

Left, scarf to cover a woman's head, called a "billum" in Iran Above, wild alpacas in Peru, S. America

WOOL

SHEARING

Using electric shears, expert workers can shear nearly 200 sheep in one day.

Above, clipping wool Right, the Masai people of Kenya, Africa, wear colorful wool clothing Opposite, wool yarn drying in Morocco

Wool repels water. Because of the fibers' scales, liquids roll off. If a person happens to get caught in a rainstorm, wool can keep its wearer dry longer than many other fibers can.

Also, wool resists dirt. Because wool can absorb wetness from the body and static electricity from outside, airborne lint and dust stay away from wool. Because of wool's scales, dirt cannot penetrate. Thus, wool is easily cleaned off.

WOOL
WEIGHT

Full bags of fleece from America weigh about 300 pounds (136 kg). Other countries ship heavier bales.

Below, bales of wool

Wool takes dyes easily and holds its color. It's **resilient** and comfortable to wear. Clothing made from it resists wrinkles and holds its shape well. Wool is also fire-resistant. It can catch on fire, but it will not blaze, and it will not keep a flame. Also, wool doesn't melt as it burns, as do more reactive synthetic fabrics. In fact, many countries use wool for their firefighters clothing.

Besides being decorative, wool used to make curtains, carpeting, and wallpaper absorbs sound. This feature of wool lowers noise levels in busy places such as airports and office buildings. Designers can use wool in concert halls to enhance sound so that orchestras and choirs give better, more rounded performances. Wool is also used in parts of speakers and amplifiers and in wall coverings of recording studios and other places that need to be made soundproof.

WOOL
TRAFFIC

Explorer Francisco Vásquez de Coronado brought sheep to America in 1540.

WOOL
MUSIC

Wool is used for the heads of sticks for bass drums and timpanis, for the pads on chimes and on the separators for hand cymbals.

Herding sheep down a highway in California

19

WOOL
L A W

Raw fleece

CLASSES OF WOOL

Before fleece is processed, it first must be sorted and graded at the woolen mill. Each bit of fleece is sorted into separate piles. Tweeds and carpets will make use of thick, short fibers. Sweaters use fine, soft wool.

Expert workers determine the different qualities of the fleece by its feel and appearance. Fleece **grades** are based on the length, fineness, stretchiness, and strength of the fleece.

WOOL
CUSHION

The Lord Chancellor of England in the House of Lords sat on a large red bag stuffed with wool called a "woolsack."

Left, dyeing fleece
Below, a Merino sheep

The workers separate the fleece into five grades, or qualities. Class One wool is also called Merino wool. This comes from Merino sheep and is considered to be the best wool. Fibers are short but strong, and they have the greatest amount of curl and scales. Merino wool is often used in high-quality clothing.

WOOL

ROYALTY

At one time, vicuñas were hunted for their fleece and nearly wiped out. Their wool was so rare and valuable that only royalty could wear it. Today, about 15,000 vicuñas exist.

WOOL

HISTORY

Centuries ago, Saxon and Viking women made socks and gloves out of wool using only bone needles and strands of yarn made by hand.

Wool is dyed in more natural colors too

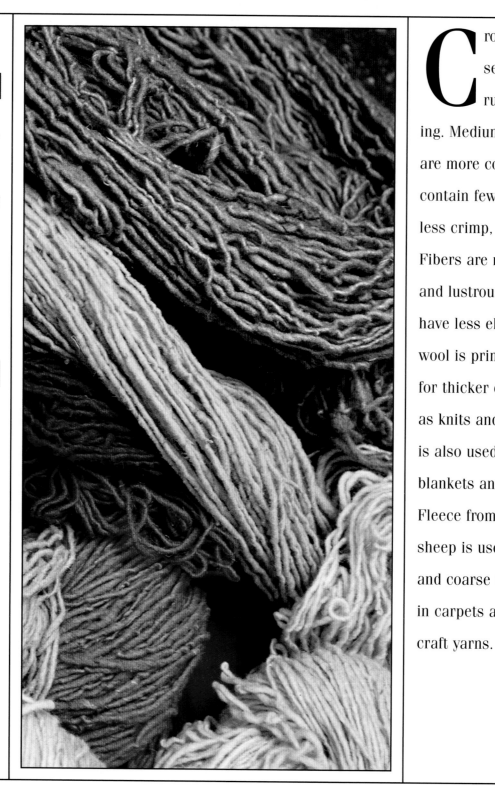

Crossbred wool serves well for rugged clothing. Medium wool fibers are more coarse and contain fewer scales and less crimp, or curl. Fibers are more smooth and lustrous, and they have less elasticity. This wool is primarily used for thicker clothing, such as knits and tweeds, and is also used to make blankets and upholstery. Fleece from long-wooled sheep is used in carpets, and coarse wool is used in carpets and handicraft yarns.

Young lambs produce softer and finer fleece than older sheep, and the feel of a first shearing differs from later ones. Another factor that affects fleece quality is whether the sheep is alive at the time of shearing. Sheep being processed for their meat are sometimes also shorn. This kind of fleece is called "pulled" wool.

One type of shearing machine removes a sheep's fleece in one sheet by cutting the wool under the sheep's belly and pulling the coat off, much like peeling an orange.

Left, knots and lumps are removed from the woven wool
Above, shorn wool is compacted for shipping

WOOL
TRIVIA

Wool from the shoulders and sides of sheep is generally better than wool from other parts of the body.

In some countries, yarn is washed and wrung out by hand

WOOL PROCESSING

Wool contains yolk, an oily material made of grease and dried perspiration, or suint. After the fleece is sorted, it must be cleaned to remove dirt, debris, and the yolk. Lanolin gathered from this cleaning process will be made into cosmetics, soaps, and lotions.

Three different systems are used in wool finishing. The **worsted** system processes longer fibers; **woolen** processing is done on shorter fibers; and lower grade leftovers are processed into felt by felting. Carding uses a large revolving cylinder with wire teeth to untangle the wool and arrange it into a thin sheet known as a web. These webs are then made into ropes called **slivers.**

The Arctic musk-ox, a large, hoofed animal, grows a deep, dense wool called "quivut." It is one of the most valuable natural fibers in the world.

Wool factories use machines to wash wool

WOOL

UNIFORM

Khaki (which means "dusty" in the Hindi language) is a durable fabric made of wool (and sometimes cotton); it was first used for uniforms by the British army in India, in 1848.

Machines also card the wool (above) and spin it into yarn (below)

Short worsted fibers are separated from the long fibers, which are then molded into compact, smooth strands. These are later spun into yarn. Because worsted fabric will plainly show its pattern, fibers are combed after carding to remove any other short fibers and to smooth the surface. The fibers may be combed over and over again until their appearance is exactly right. Then the yarn is woven or knitted. Worsted yarn is smooth; its fabric is used for fine suits of clothes and hosiery.

WOOL

F A C T

In the late 1700s, Boston became the leading wool market for the industry. Today, American whole-sale wool prices are still set in Boston.

Left, bobbin and spools used in Harris tweeds Below, traditional wool yarns and tools used in Navajo weaving

For woolens, fibers are carded and then spun. No combing is done. Woolens have a more bulky, fuzzy appearance than worsteds. Woolen fibers make up blankets, flannel, overcoats, and sweaters.

In felting, wool fibers are padded together in a warm, soapy solution. The fibers mat together into felt, which is often used for sewing and crafts.

WOOL

PREHISTORY

Long ago, people "ironed" wool cloth by rubbing it between a flat whale bone and a large stone that had been heated in hot sand.

28

MAKING FABRIC

Both woolens and worsteds are pulled into a fine strand by a process called roving. The strand itself is known as a roving too, and it is wound around a **bobbin** where it can be spun. Electric machines take the fibers and pull them into single strands. Several strands are twisted into yarns. Wool can be dyed at any point in its processing, when it is yarn or after it is made into fabric.

Factories weave fabric at high speeds

VOCABULARY

For hundreds of years in Europe, the word "rug" meant any rough, heavy, woolen fabric with a coarse, napped finish and used as clothing by the poorer citizens.

Huge looms make cloth in various widths

The yarns are then processed according to whether they are meant to be coarse or smooth, long or short, woven into fabric, or knitted. **Skeins** of yarn for knitting are gathered into bales and shipped off to knitting mills. This yarn is used to make clothing, including sweaters and scarves. The bales of yarn that are used to make fabric move on to large, automatic **looms,** where the threads are woven in solid colors or in patterns.

30

Right, finished fabrics are wrapped into large rolls called "bolts" Opposite, wool has a long history all around the world

Worsted and woolen fabrics receive either a clear finish or a face finish. In a clear finish the fabric is given a smooth surface by cutting it closely to remove all the bumps of the woven yarns. The weave of the fabric is easy to see. Face finishing raises the **nap** of the fabric so that it looks thick and fuzzy.

Any remaining soap residue is washed out, and the fabric is shrunk to its desired length using hot water and rollers. Then the cloth is dried. If there is a nap in the fabric, it is combed out again.

inally, the cloth is trimmed to size and pressed. It is then ready to be made into clothing or many other products.

For thousands of years, people around the world have harvested the fleece of sheep, goats, camels, and rabbits to create dozens of things, from warm sweaters to thick socks. Whether it's traditional handwoven Navajo blankets or machine-made carpeting, wool touches nearly every part of our daily lives. It is a natural, renewable resource that will continue to be used for years to come.

Glossary

A material has **absorbency** if it can take in and hold water.

A **bobbin** is a reel or spool that holds yarn for spinning or weaving.

When wool fleece is untangled and turned into one continuous strand it is **carded.**

Domesticated sheep are those raised on farms, as opposed to wild sheep that roam free.

Grades are classes ranging from very good to less desirable. Wool has five grades, each with different uses.

Guanacos are non-domesticated mammals related to the llama; they live in South America.

A country that **imports** goods and products from another country has purchased them to sell in its own country.

Like several other fabrics, wool **insulates,** meaning that it protects against very cold or very hot temperatures.

Fabric has a **nap** if its surface is fuzzy.

The **Navajo** are a group of Native American people from northern New Mexico and Arizona.

Perspiration is another word for sweat; mammals cool down when perspiration evaporates from the skin.

A material is **resilient** if it is strong and able to withstand wear and tear.

To **shear** is to shave a sheep or another animal of its fleece.

Slivers (SLY-vers) are ropes of wool before they are finished.

Woolen fibers are those that have been carded and then spun.

Worsted fibers are those that have been carded and then combed to separate the long fibers from the short ones. They are then made into yarn and later, fabric.

Index